For Your Wedding

CENTERPIECES

AND TABLE ACCENTS

For Your Wedding

CENTERPIECES

AND TABLE ACCENTS

Kathy Passero

BARNES
& NOBLE
BOOKS
NEW YORK

A BARNES & NOBLE BOOK

First paperback edition 2004

©2002 by Michael Friedman Publishing Group, Inc.

ISBN 0-7607-5540-X

Front cover photograph: ©Andrea Sperling (floral design by Susan Holland, NYC)

Color separations by Fine Arts Repro House Co., Ltd.
Printed and bound in China by C&C Printing Co., Ltd.

1 3 5 7 9 10 8 6 4 2

CONTENTS

INTRODUCTION

*F*ew sights are as inviting as a table that has been beautifully set—bathed in soft candlelight, sparkling with crystal, and crowned by a captivating centerpiece. Nothing sets the stage more perfectly for a delicious meal full of lively conversation, laughter, and warmth. And perhaps nowhere is the effect more profound than at a wedding.

Family and friends will arrive at your reception still glowing from the joy of sharing in your ceremony. As they look around eagerly for their tables, the first items to capture their attention will undoubtedly be the centerpieces. What better way to welcome guests and create a riveting first impression than with a cornucopia of colorful flowers, tantalizing fruit, and lush greenery?

Long after a wedding, guests often remember the centerpieces. After all, these adornments are literally at the center of the dining experience, providing a visual treat as guests listen to heartfelt toasts, make new acquaintances, catch up with old friends, and linger over sinfully rich desserts. Many people become so captivated by the centerpieces that when the reception ends, they take one home—to savor the arrangement's beauty for a few more days or, perhaps, to re-create the composition in silk flowers, which can be enjoyed as a memento of the happy occasion for years to come.

Centerpieces not only enhance the festive spirit of a wedding reception, but also provide a unique way for a bride and groom to express their sense of style. With a bit of imagination and the help of a knowledgeable florist, you can use flowers and other forms of ornamentation to help define any decorative theme. If your taste leans toward Shakespearean romance, you might choose cascades of velvety scarlet roses spilling over golden candelabra. If you favor the casual charm of a country garden, you might tuck an assortment of fresh-picked wildflowers and sweet-scented lavender into burnished copper kettles or oversize china teacups. Those who prefer minimalist chic might select all-white tables, each adorned with a single orchid in a sleek crystal vase.

Today, flowers are used in weddings primarily for their beauty. But the tradition began long ago, when brides in ancient Greece placed flowers in their hair and scattered grains along the bridal path as a tribute to the gods, hoping to be blessed with an abundant, prosperous future. Orange blossoms, considered the symbol of undying love thanks to their ability to bloom all year, were among the favorites.

PAGE 6: GLEAMING SILVER VESSELS—TIGHTLY PACKED WITH PASTEL BLOOMS—ARE PAIRED WITH WHITE CANDLES IN CYLINDRICAL HOLDERS, GIVING THIS TABLE AN ALLURING GLOW. ALTHOUGH EACH BOUQUET IS UNIQUE, ALL ARE COMPLEMENTARY IN TERMS OF STYLE AND COLOR TO CONVEY A SENSE OF UNITY.

OPPOSITE: AN EXQUISITE CENTERPIECE COMPOSED OF 'GRAND PRIX' ROSES, HYDRANGEAS, MINIATURE CALLA LILIES, AND VIBURNUM MAKES AN ELEGANT FOCAL POINT FOR THIS TABLE. RICH SHADES OF RED AND BURGUNDY IMBUE THE ARRANGEMENT WITH AN AIR OF SENSUALITY. AT EACH PLACE SETTING, DELICATE HYDRANGEA FLORETS AWAIT GUESTS.

OPPOSITE: A WIREWORK
TEAPOT PLAYS HOST TO A
SPRINGLIKE ARRANGEMENT
OF LILACS, GERBERA DAISIES,
DAFFODILS, AND QUEEN
ANNE'S LACE. MATCHING
TEACUPS BRIMMING WITH
MANY OF THE SAME FLOWERS
COMPLETE THE VIGNETTE.

Greek mythology holds that Hera—goddess of marriage and childbirth—received them when she married Zeus.

Thousands of years later, Queen Victoria rekindled the orange blossom's popularity by wearing a garland of these blooms as part of her bridal ensemble. In fact, it was the Victorians, with their fondness for opulent decoration, who took the use of wedding flowers to new heights. Petals were strewn lavishly down aisles and over altars, while arches and doorways were embellished with magnificent wreaths. Every surface was adorned—including the tables.

Of course, women marrying during Queen Victoria's reign would have been bewildered by many of today's centerpieces—some of which don't even contain flowers. Contemporary offerings include unstructured displays, with flowers loosely arranged in asymmetrical vases; whimsical antique tea sets, filled with decorative potpourri; and miniature wooden boats, trimmed with nautical blue and white bows. Such unusual designs would have raised eyebrows even fifty years ago, when white was de rigueur for brides and tables were decked with traditional arrangements—round in shape and featuring flowers as their mainstay.

In the late 1960s, however, a trend emerged toward more innovative weddings. Couples exchanged vows on mountaintops with spiritual gurus presiding, acoustic guitars for processional music, and Native American poetry in lieu of Scripture. Personal expression took precedence over established convention.

Since then, weddings have become even more inventive. Today, a couple might let their love of the Jazz Age guide not only their wedding's music but also the decorative motif, perhaps incorporating centerpieces of ivory calla lilies,

which were popular in the 1920s. Or, if both bride and groom adore nineteenth-century English literature, they might include a reading from Emily Brontë's *Wuthering Heights* in the ceremony and design centerpieces based on the Victorian custom of attributing romantic meanings to different flowers (jasmine for joy, bluebells for constancy, and so on), with a decoratively framed explanation placed on each table.

The more specific you can be about your vision of the perfect centerpiece, the more likely it is that you and your florist will be able to bring your dream to life. Save photographs from magazines and books to illustrate what you find most appealing in terms of color, types of flowers, containers, and overall style—as well as what you want to avoid with respect to these different areas. And don't limit your creative powers to just the center of the table; the decorative theme can be extended with flower petals scattered gently about or with an individual bloom, fruit, or shiny bauble set atop each plate.

As you gather ideas, remember that the style of your centerpieces should harmonize with the other aspects of your wedding. Ornate urns with towering pyramids of flowers would be jarring at a casual outdoor brunch; similarly, rustic baskets of apples and mums would seem out of place at a sophisticated black-tie dinner.

Aesthetics are not the only consideration, though, when it comes to deciding upon centerpieces. Practical concerns, such as seasonality, also come into play. If you're planning a winter wedding, for instance, summer bloomers such as bougainvillea and honeysuckle may be scarce. Though today's nurseries cultivate

OPPOSITE: FLOWERS NEED NOT BE CONFINED TO THE CENTER OF THE TABLE. HERE, A PALE PINK ROSEBUD IS SECURED TO A SQUARE OF WHITE ORGANZA, CREATING A CHARMING NAPKIN RING.

OPPOSITE: THOUGH AT FIRST
GLANCE THIS LUXURIANT
TANGLE OF COLORFUL BLOOMS
APPEARS TO BE A SINGLE
BOUQUET, IT IS ACTUALLY
A BREAKAWAY CENTERPIECE
DESIGNED TO OFFER EACH
FEMALE GUEST A FLORAL
KEEPSAKE. HIDDEN AMONG
THE GRAPES, KUMQUATS,
AND ARTICHOKES ARE FIVE
SMALL POTS OVERFLOWING
WITH CHINESE PEONIES,
SCABIOSA, DUTCH SWEET PEAS,
NEW ZEALAND HYDRANGEA,
HYPERICUM BERRIES, AND
A VARIETY OF ROSES.

many plants year-round, out-of-season flowers tend to be costly. Ask your florist what will be in season at the time of your wedding; not only will these blossoms be more affordable, they will be at their fullest and most glorious as well. Florists can often suggest alternatives that closely resemble your out-of-season favorites.

Keep in mind, too, that certain blossoms are highly sensitive to heat and cold, so if you're planning an outdoor summer wedding, avoid such fragile blooms as gardenias, which wilt easily in humid weather. Other flowers produce strong scents that can affect the ability to taste food.

Finally, stick to your budget. While using in-season flowers is one way of keeping expenses in line, a good florist should be able to offer a number of creative options that will bring the cost down without sacrificing beauty. If you love the lush look of red roses but can't afford bundles of them, your florist might propose interspersing a limited number with ruby red pears, pomegranates, and flowers that are less expensive but equally rich in color and texture. Another economical option is to use breakaway centerpieces—separate, small bouquets that are potted and clustered together to create the effect of one large center-piece. The individual components can double as favors, with each guest taking a diminutive arrangement home after the reception.

In the following pages, you'll find an abundance of refreshing ideas for cen-terpieces that will bring style and originality to your celebration. These examples are just the beginning—a way to spark your imagination and encourage you to dream, envision, and invent.

CHAPTER ONE

COLOR AND TEXTURE

Nature offers an almost endless palette of colors, and virtually every one of these hues can bring beauty to a centerpiece—from the most delicate pastel yellow or pistachio to the richest ruby, amber, or emerald. Some couples even draw inspiration from an absence of color, creating a look of sophisticated simplicity with purely white arrangements.

When choosing a color scheme for your centerpieces, consider the different types of hues and their effects. Do you want to make a bold statement with such deep hues as daring reds, vivid purples, or brilliant fuchsia? Or does your taste run toward something much softer, more subdued—perhaps creamy white or the slightest whisper of pink? Perhaps the answer for you lies somewhere in between, with a medium hue such as peach.

RIGHT: A SILVER CONTAINER
OVERFLOWING WITH RED ROSES
SPEAKS OF ROMANCE AND
PASSION. COMPOSED ENTIRELY
OF THESE LUXURIOUS FLOWERS,
THE EVOCATIVE BOUQUET SEEMS
ALMOST DECADENT.

OPPOSITE: QUIET AND
SUBDUED, THE SOFT WHITES
AND PASTELS OF THESE
FLOWERS OFFER A LOOK OF
UNDERSTATED REFINEMENT.
A SMOOTH SILVER BOWL,
A PAIR OF WHITE VOTIVES,
AND A SMATTERING OF LOOSE
PETALS ENHANCE THE EFFECT.

RIGHT: OPULENT JEWEL TONES INCLUDING PURPLE AND CANARY YELLOW COMBINE IN A MAGNIFICENT EXPLOSION OF COLOR ON THIS HEAD TABLE, ACCENTED BY GOLD LINENS AND BLOCKY GEOMETRIC CANDLES INLAID WITH LEAVES. THE EYE-CATCHING ARRAY OF COLORS SETS THIS SPECIAL TABLE APART FROM THE OTHERS, WHICH ARE ADORNED WITH MONO-CHROMATIC ARRANGEMENTS.

OPPOSITE: A SILVER BOWL FILLED WITH TAUPE ROSES IS BOTH SIMPLE AND ELEGANT. THE CREAMY TONES OF THE DAMASK TABLE LINENS UNDER-SCORE THE TOASTED-ALMOND HUE OF THE FLOWERS, WHILE ADDITIONAL TOUCHES OF SILVER, SUCH AS THE CANDLESTICKS AND THE SMALL BELLS SITUATED AT EACH PLACE SETTING, ROUND OUT THE TABLEAU.

Picture the different possibilities and the responses that they elicit. A couple who favors intense color and drama might opt for baskets of gold-and-burgundy Swiss pansies, robust purple orchids, and orange tulips, or maybe grand sprays of scarlet cockscomb and amaryllis. Either one of these arrangements is bound to inject a table with vitality. Couples who prefer less saturated colors will find attractive options in the medium family—imagine a profusion of lavender sweet peas and blue delphiniums designed to infuse the table with the charm of a country garden. Those who wish to set a tone of understated elegance might deck their tables with vases of roses and peonies in muted shades of blush pink and café au lait or fill cachepots with arrangements of pale yellow daffodils and ivory hyacinths.

OPPOSITE: AN ABUNDANCE OF ROSES IN SHADES RANGING FROM PALE PEACH TO BURNT SIENNA GIVES THIS TABLE AN AUTUMNAL GLOW, WHICH IS REINFORCED BY A GOLD SCALLOPED BOWL, GOLD-FLECKED VOTIVE HOLDERS, AND AUBURN TABLE LINENS. FOR ADDED ELEGANCE, A SINGLE ROSEBUD AND A DECORATIVE MENU ARE TUCKED INTO EACH NAPKIN, WHICH IS IN TURN WRAPPED IN SATIN RIBBON. WHILE THE OVERALL LOOK IS SUMPTUOUS, THE DISPLAY MAINTAINS A CERTAIN SIM-PLICITY, THANKS TO THE USE OF ONE TYPE OF FLOWER AND GRADATIONS OF ONE COLOR.

LEFT: A BOUNTY OF GLORIOUS ROSES BRIMS OVER A SILVER BOWL, PROVIDING A STUDY IN CONTRASTING SHADES OF RED—FROM SOFT ORANGE TO BOLD CRIMSON.

It's also possible to design beautiful centerpieces by combining several color categories. For example, a tall crystal vase filled with red and white tulips creates a dynamic two-tone effect. Summery yellow buttercups pair with midnight blue cornflowers to evoke the lighthearted appeal of bouquets freshly gathered from a meadow. Silver serving bowls packed with roses in gradations of orange, from deep auburn to soft apricot, produce a chic monochromatic look, which has become quite popular in recent years.

Another important factor to consider when choosing centerpieces is texture. Although color is more obvious at first glance, spend some time browsing through a flower market and you'll soon discover remarkable differences in the textures of various flowers. Ranunculus petals, for instance, are as delicate as tissue paper,

RIGHT: ROSES, RANUNCULUSES, AND OTHER BLOOMS—ALL IN SHADES OF RED, YELLOW, AND WHITE—COMBINE WITH GENEROUS CLUSTERS OF PALE GREEN HYDRANGEAS AND LACY VIBURNUM TO PRODUCE A DENSE TAPESTRY OF FLOWERS. THE COMPLEX TEXTURES AND CONTRASTING COLORS EVOKE A SENSE OF SHAKESPEAREAN ROMANCE, ENHANCED BY THE STATELY PEDESTAL BOWL WITH ITS NEOCLASSICAL LINES AND ANTIQUED-SILVER FINISH.

OPPOSITE: A LAVISH GATHERING OF LILACS, VIBURNUM, ROSES, AND GLORIOSA LILIES CREATES A PROFUSION OF WARMTH AND TEXTURE. WHILE MOST OF THE FLOWERS SELECTED COME FROM THE SAME COLOR FAMILY, PASTELS MINGLE WITH DEEPER SHADES TO PROVIDE DRAMA AND CONTRAST. RINGED WITH GLOWING CANDLES AND PLACED ON A DARK TABLECLOTH, THE CENTERPIECE LOOKS UTTERLY ROMANTIC. PLACE SETTINGS ARRANGED QUITE CLOSE TO ONE ANOTHER ENHANCE THE SENSE OF INTIMACY.

while peonies are ruffled, resembling the sleeves of certain bridal gowns. Lilacs, with their many tiny blossoms clinging together, create an intricate lacelike effect—a striking contrast to the sculpted simplicity of calla lilies. Likewise, stephanotis and magnolias, with their waxy blossoms, produce an entirely different look than violets and pansies, which have a velvety texture.

Much more than its color, a flower's texture and shape naturally express certain design aesthetics. Hence, just as a bride who prefers a pared-down sense of elegance might wear a simple, sleeveless shantung gown and plan a reception in a modern penthouse, she might also select blossoms with clean lines and unfussy textures—such as calla lilies, tulips, and unassuming white jasmine blossoms. Such flowers would be in keeping with both her sense of style and the look of the reception site. The bride who favors a brocade gown and a castle setting might find that more ornate blooms, such as peonies and lilacs, better capture her penchant for Elizabethan romance.

OPPOSITE: IVY TRAILS FROM A SILVER CANDELABRUM HOLDING FOUR IVORY TAPERS. ALTHOUGH DOTTED WITH A SMATTERING OF PINK AND PURPLE FLOWERS, THE CENTER-PIECE CLEARLY EMPHASIZES SHADES OF GREEN AND WHITE. THIS SUBTLE COLOR SCHEME IS REPEATED, WITH THE ADDI-TION OF GOLD, IN THE UNUSUAL CHARGERS, EACH DESIGNED AS THE FACE OF A CLOCK.

LEFT: WITH ITS VARIEGATED GREEN LEAVES, ITALIAN PITTOSPORUM ADDS A TOUCH OF PIZZAZZ TO AN ARRANGEMENT OF HYDRANGEAS, ROSES, LISIANTHUS, DELPHINIUMS, AND LILACS.

Greenery provides a lovely and cost-effective way to add texture and fullness to any centerpiece. Victorians saw ivy as a symbol of fidelity, and this plant's distinctive vines still grace many wedding tables, trailing from baskets and tumbling down candelabra to achieve a look of lush abundance. Other perpetual favorites include sprays of fragrant eucalyptus, frothy helxine, and summery wheatgrass. Some couples dispense with flowers altogether in favor of centerpieces composed entirely of vibrant greenery.

RIGHT: WITH ITS AUTUMNAL HUES, A CENTERPIECE FEATURING ROSES, PARROT TULIPS, PEPPER-BERRIES, AND LADY APPLES PROVIDES A FITTING ACCENT FOR AN OCTOBER WEDDING.

OPPOSITE: SHADES OF GREEN, CREAM, AND WHITE MERGE IN THIS REFRESHING ARRANGE-MENT OF 'LIMONA' ROSES, LISIANTHUS, AND SPIREA. SLICED LIMES AND KIWIS PLACED IN AND AROUND THE CENTERPIECE PROVIDE CHARMING COUNTER-POINTS TO THE LONG, LACY STALKS OF BELLS OF IRELAND AND AMARANTHUS. WHOLE LIMES ARE ALSO INCLUDED, THEIR DIMPLED GREEN SKINS BRINGING ADDITIONAL TEXTURE TO THE MIX.

Another way of adding intriguing texture, as well as color, to a centerpiece is by incorporating fruits and vegetables. Many of today's floral designers are weaving these natural elements in between blossoms and leaves, thereby heightening the visual interest of the arrangement. What a delightful surprise for guests to discover halves of kiwi popping up amid the leafy greenery of a centerpiece. And think of the added flair that plump strawberries would lend to a monochromatic display of red blooms.

OPPOSITE: A BLISSFUL UNION OF FLOWERS AND FRUIT FEATURES ALMOST EVERY COLOR OF THE RAINBOW. PEEKING OUT FROM AMONG THE DAHLIAS, ROSES, ASTILBE, LISIANTHUS, AND LADY'S MANTLE ARE LEMONS, LIMES, NECTARINES, STRAWBERRIES, RED GRAPES, AND OTHER GIFTS OF A BOUNTIFUL HARVEST. ASPARAGUS SPEARS POP UP HERE AND THERE, PROVIDING A WHIMSICAL TOUCH.

LEFT: SPLASHES OF INTENSE FUCHSIA, BURGUNDY, AND VIOLET MAKE A POWERFUL STATEMENT ATOP A WHITE TABLE. THIS ARRESTING DISPLAY MIXES PEONIES, LISIANTHUS, SWEET PEAS, AND STOCK WITH WHEATGRASS, SHINY ORANGE KUMQUATS, AND RIPE RED STRAWBERRIES, ALL OF WHICH LOOK AS THOUGH THEY WERE PLUCKED FROM THE RECEPTION'S GARDEN SETTING THAT MORNING. FLAMBOYANT AND INNOVATIVE, THE ARRANGEMENT IS MEANT TO TAKE CENTER STAGE, WITH SURROUNDING ELEMENTS DECIDEDLY UNDERPLAYED.

If you're finding it difficult to pick just one type of centerpiece, consider making each arrangement unique. For example, one group of guests might be treated to a basket of buttery yellow and gold mums, while another group is given a basket brimming with burgundy and crimson mums. For a different twist, keep the color consistent but vary the type of flower—sprays of white roses for one table, white lilacs for another, and so on. Note that both examples weave a unifying design element through every arrangement.

Remember that your centerpieces should blend with other elements of your reception—not only the linens and china, but the architectural and decorative style of the setting. This doesn't mean that ornate locales require over-the-top centerpieces. On the contrary, lavish, multicolored floral arrangements in a baroque dining room can look chaotic and dizzying. By contrast, monochromatic cream centerpieces might appear washed-out in a room of subdued beige walls and linens. So keep the look of the backdrop in mind as you settle upon a color scheme.

LEFT: A CLOSE-UP OF ONE OF
THE CENTERPIECES REVEALS
A DAZZLING DISPLAY OF
YELLOW CALLA LILIES AND
TULIPS IN THE MIDST OF GREEN
AMARANTHUS AND CLUSTERS
OF TINY BURGUNDY BLOSSOMS.

LEFT: A MASS OF ORANGE ROSES
AND CALLA LILIES, DOTTED WITH
CLUSTERS OF THE SAME INTRI-
CATELY TEXTURED BURGUNDY
BLOSSOMS, FILLS A SILVER PLATE
FRAMED BY CANDLES.

RIGHT: FOR AN OUTDOOR RECEPTION ON A SUMMER AFTERNOON, A CRISP GREEN AND WHITE CENTERPIECE CONSISTING OF IVORY 'ICEBERG' GARDEN ROSES, SPRAY ROSES, AND WHITE PHLOX IS PLACED ATOP A SIMPLY PATTERNED WHITE LINEN TABLECLOTH. THE LOOK IS NOT QUITE MONOCHROMATIC, THANKS TO THE GREENERY TUCKED IN AMONG THE FLOWERS. SUCH GREENERY PROVIDES A VISUAL LINK BETWEEN THE TABLE AND THE TREE-LINED FIELD IT OVER-LOOKS, JUST AS THE PATTERN OF THE BLACK WIRE BASKET HOLD-ING THE ARRANGEMENT TIES IN WITH THE BALCONY'S RAILING.

OPPOSITE: A GATHERING OF PEONIES, ROSES, AND VIBURNUM TUMBLES OVER THE RIM OF A PAINTED CHINESE EXPORT VASE. THE FLORAL ARRANGEMENT'S EBULLIENT MIXTURE OF PALE PEACH, SOFT PINK, LIME GREEN, AND VIBRANT ORANGE COM-PLEMENTS THE YELLOW, BLUE, AND PINK ARTWORK ON THE CONTAINER, CREATING AN UPLIFTING DISPLAY OF COLOR. FOR A COMPLETELY COHESIVE EFFECT, THE VIVID CORAL PEONIES ECHO THE HUE OF THE FLOWERS GROWING IN THE GARDEN SETTING.

CHAPTER TWO

SHAPE AND STYLE

PAGE 38: AN EXTRAVAGANT
ARRANGEMENT OF TULIPS
SURROUNDED BY FOUR
ELEVATED TAPERS HEIGHTENS
THE SENSE OF GRANDEUR AT
A FORMAL RECEPTION.

OPPOSITE: AN ARRANGEMENT
OF PEONIES, LILIES, ROSES,
AND IRISES IN A CHEER-
FUL PALETTE OF PINKS AND
PURPLES CONJURES IMAGES
OF SPRINGTIME. THE SIMPLE
VASE AND VISIBLE STEMS
SUGGEST A RELAXED, LIGHT-
HEARTED OCCASION.

LEFT: AN ASSORTMENT OF
UNUSUALLY SHAPED CANDLES
AND SMALL VASES, EACH TIGHTLY
PACKED WITH FLOWERS OF A
DIFFERENT TYPE AND COLOR,
YIELDS A MEMORABLE TABLEAU.
THE STRONG GEOMETRIC FORMS
OF BOTH THE CANDLES AND
VASES UNIFIES THE MÉLANGE
OF CONTRASTING ELEMENTS.
MODERN AND STYLISH,
THIS UNIQUE CENTERPIECE
UNDOUBTEDLY REFLECTS
THE BRIDE'S INDIVIDUAL
SENSE OF DESIGN.

*S*erving as focal points, your centerpieces play a large role in establishing the

desired tone of your reception. Thankfully, today's offerings are as varied as the

tastes of the couples selecting them. And since the wide range of compositions

allows for every possible aesthetic and mood, you should make the most of these

celebratory adornments and treat them as personal expressions of style.

RIGHT: DIMINUTIVE SILK POUCHES OF ROSES AND LOW VOTIVES NOT ONLY BATHE A TABLE IN ROMANCE, BUT ALSO ALLOW GUESTS TO SEE ONE ANOTHER EASILY.

OPPOSITE: THIS TABLE HAS STRATEGICALLY BEEN ADORNED SO THAT EACH GUEST CAN FULLY ENJOY THE BEAUTY OF A FLORAL ARRANGEMENT, REGARDLESS OF WHERE HE OR SHE IS SITTING. A BRUSHED-CHROME CANDELABRUM—RINGED WITH PINK, PURPLE, AND WHITE BLOSSOMS AT TOP AND BOTTOM—SHINES IN THE CENTER OF THE RECTANGULAR TABLE, WHILE MATCHING LOW DOMES OF FLOWERS APPEAR ON EITHER SIDE. USING MULTIPLE CANDELABRA WOULD HAVE OVERWHELMED THE TABLE, BUT THE PRESENT DESIGN CREATES A SENSE OF BALANCE.

But before you explore the myriad options available, it is best to have a grasp of certain basics with respect to the forms that centerpieces can take. Regardless of your style preference, you'll want to make sure that the centerpieces you select don't prevent your guests from seeing their tablemates. No matter how breathtaking the decorative display, it should not force diners to slouch in their seats or crane their necks to make conversation with the people sitting across from them. In order to avoid this problem and ensure visibility, centerpieces usually adhere to one of two general forms: low or tall arrangements.

RIGHT: AN EASY-TO-SEE-OVER DOME OF PINK, YELLOW, AND RED ROSES IS SURROUNDED BY WHITE CYLINDRICAL CANDLES. SET ATOP A TABLE COVERED IN CREAMS AND WHITES, THE COLORFUL FLORAL ARRANGEMENT IMMEDIATELY DRAWS THE EYE.

OPPOSITE: A BANK OF SUN-FLOWERS, LILIES, BELLS OF IRELAND, DAHLIAS, AND SNAP-DRAGONS SIMULATES THE UNTAMED APPEAL OF AN OVER-GROWN GARDEN. PLUS, THE ARRANGEMENT'S LOW PROFILE ENSURES THAT FRIENDS AND RELATIVES HAVE UNOBSTRUCTED VIEWS OF ONE ANOTHER. THE LUSH LOOK IS ENHANCED BY LEAF-PATTERNED CHINA AND BEGONIAS SITUATED AT EACH PLACE SETTING.

Low arrangements sit comfortably below guests' sight lines, with the tallest flowers extending no more than fourteen inches (36cm) above the table. The classic low centerpiece is dome-shaped—a whiteware bowl, for example, packed with sunflowers and marigolds for a summer afternoon reception. In another version of a low design, flowers and greenery appear to lie directly on the table, thanks to their deft arrangement in a camouflaged tray. More vertical approaches might include decorative pitchers with fanlike sprays of snapdragons and bells of Ireland, clusters of votive candles interspersed with silver bud vases, or rustic wooden boxes of narcissus.

RIGHT: LONG-STEMMED FLOW-
ERS IN A SVELTE VASE FORM A
LAVISH DISPLAY WELL ABOVE
THE HEADS OF SEATED GUESTS.
THE PRACTICAL DESIGN ALLOWS
GUESTS TO SAVOR THE BEAUTY
OF THE BLOOMS WITHOUT
INTERFERING WITH THEIR
ENJOYMENT OF THE EVENING.

OPPOSITE: THANKS TO ITS
TWO-TIER DESIGN, THIS
CENTERPIECE ALLOWS CON-
VERSATION TO FLOW FREELY.
MUTED PASTEL FLOWERS RING
THE BASE OF THE CANDE-
LABRUM, WHILE GREENERY AND
WHITE ROSES WIND THEIR WAY
UP TOWARD SIX IVORY TAPERS
HELD ALOFT—ABOVE THE EYE
LEVEL OF SEATED GUESTS.

Tall arrangements feature slender bases that hold flowers above a seated guest's line of vision or some other design that is narrow enough to let guests see easily around it. The most traditional tall centerpieces involve candelabra, often used to create a two-tier effect with one wreath of flowers around the base and another atop the stem, where the tapers are inserted. Among the variations are tabletop topiaries with narrow trunks supporting spheres of roses and statuesque pyramids of flowers and fruit.

In today's world of wedding planning, where individual preferences reign supreme, you need not be limited to one type of arrangement. To create drama and visual rhythm, many brides intersperse short and tall centerpieces, adorning some tables with low dome-shaped compositions and others with lofty candelabra draped in similar flowers.

Just like the color scheme, the size of your centerpieces should work in harmony with your reception's setting. Hence, shorter arrangements are ideal for cozy, low-ceilinged rooms, such as those of historic cottages and inns. Tall centerpieces, by contrast, are most striking in lofts, ballrooms, and other locations with soaring ceilings. Both styles can be used at formal and informal weddings, though some containers and flowers lend themselves more naturally to one or the other.

OPPOSITE: AN ORNATE CRYSTAL CANDELABRUM IS DECKED WITH A MAGNIFICENT ARRAY OF BLOOMS. WHILE SUCH A MAJESTIC CENTERPIECE MIGHT OVERPOWER A SMALLER SETTING, IT WORKS WELL IN THIS SPACIOUS BALLROOM.

ABOVE: ALTERNATING BETWEEN HIGH AND LOW CENTERPIECES LENDS AN AIR OF EXCITEMENT TO A BLACK-TIE EVENT. WHILE THE ELEVATED BOUQUETS WORK IN HARMONY WITH THE ROOM'S SOARING CEILING AND WINDOWS, THE LOW ARRANGEMENTS MAINTAIN A SENSE OF INTIMACY.

RIGHT: A WOODLAND GATHER-
ING OF SCABIOSA, VERONICA,
DATES, BELLADONNA, SPRAY
ROSES, ROSEMARY, AND PHLOX
MAINTAINS THE CASUAL MOOD
OF THIS OUTDOOR AFFAIR,
WHICH IS ALSO OUTFITTED WITH
RUSTIC, TEXTURED TABLECLOTHS
AND MODEST PLACE SETTINGS.
THE CHEERFUL PURPLE, PINK,
AND YELLOW BLOSSOMS LOOK
AS THOUGH THEY MIGHT HAVE
BEEN HANDPICKED FROM A
FOREST PATH NEARBY.

OPPOSITE: A ROUGH WOODEN
CRATE WITH A ROPE BORDER
MAKES A FITTING HOME FOR
A GROUPING OF DAISIES,
QUEEN ANNE'S LACE, AND
WHEATGRASS. THE INFORMAL
LOOK IS ENHANCED BY SAND-
AND-SHELL-FILLED VOTIVES
THAT CONTRIBUTE TO THE
RELAXED AMBIENCE. TOGETHER,
THE DECORATIVE ELEMENTS
SUGGEST A SEASIDE SETTING
LOCATED NEAR A STRETCH OF
UNSPOILED COUNTRYSIDE.

Candelabra, for example, suggest formality, while daisies and wheatgrass evoke a sweet simplicity better suited to casual celebrations.

It's also important to keep your centerpieces in proportion to the tables. A diminutive china teacup of violets would seem dwarfed atop a table large enough to seat twelve guests for a sit-down dinner, while informal cocktail tables for four would be overwhelmed by grandiose bouquets with trails of ivy that leave little room for plates and glasses.

OPPOSITE: WOODEN CHAIRS
AND TINTED TUMBLERS SUGGEST
A STYLISH BUT EASYGOING
ATMOSPHERE, REINFORCED
BY MOUNDS OF ORANGE
ECUADORIAN ROSES DOTTING
THE LONG TABLE. ELONGATED
LEAVES STRETCH OUT IN VARIOUS
DIRECTIONS LIKE NEW SHOOTS
OF GREENERY, CREATING AN
ENERGIZING EFFECT.

LEFT: A COMPACT, DOME-SHAPED
ARRANGEMENT OF PINKISH
PURPLE ROSES LENDS AN AIR
OF REFINEMENT TO A CONTEM-
PORARY SETTING. LINENS IN
FLATTERING SHADES OF PURPLE
WERE CAREFULLY SELECTED TO
WORK WITH THE FLOWERS.

In addition to height, centerpieces can be grouped into two categories based on the general way in which their flowers are arranged—tightly packed or loosely configured. Each has a profoundly different effect on the overall impact of the blooms.

Tightly packed bouquets are composed of many blossoms clustered together to generate a profusion of color, texture, or both. With this type of grouping, a bride might create anything from a casual arrangement of antique watering cans bursting with blue hydrangeas, grape hyacinths, and briar roses to a perfectly ordered semi-circle of red roses in a shiny silver bowl.

Loosely arranged centerpieces call attention to the structure, shape, and color of individual flowers. For a reception held in a modern art gallery, branches of yellow forsythia might be placed in large stone vases to produce a strikingly contemporary design. A couple celebrating their wedding on a family farm might drape tables in colorful linens and top them with black-eyed Susans and goldenrod tossed loosely into baskets to give the appearance of wildflowers picked during a country stroll.

Using these basic shapes, you can create an almost limitless number of centerpiece designs, ranging from classically elegant to avant-garde. Your choice should reflect your unique sense of style rather than merely reproduce an existing bouquet. However, well-known decorative styles often prove to be helpful sources of inspiration. Descriptions of these follow in order to help get you started.

OPPOSITE: ORANGE AND YELLOW TULIPS, VANDA ORCHIDS, ANEMONES, RANUNCULUSES, AND QUEEN ANNE'S LACE ARE LOOSELY ARRANGED TO PRODUCE A CHIC, CONTEMPORARY LOOK. NOTE THE MANY VERTICAL SHAPES—THE GLASS VASE, THE TALL WISPY FLOWERS, AND THE NAPKINS TUCKED INTO THE GOBLETS—ALL OF WHICH CREATE A SCULPTED EFFECT. TRADITIONAL ENGLISH CRACKERS SET ATOP EACH BREAD PLATE DO DOUBLE DUTY AS FAVORS AND PLACE MARKERS.

LEFT: WITH ITS USE OF BRILLIANT COLORS AND SENSUOUS TEXTURES, THIS SUMPTUOUS JUMBLE OF 'KONFETTI' ROSES, CHOCOLATE COSMOS, AND RIPE FRUIT SEEMS TO DRAW INSPIRATION FROM THE STILL LIFES OF THE OLD MASTERS. WHILE THE EFFECT IS LAVISH, THE CENTERPIECE SEEMS NONETHELESS TO FIT RIGHT IN AT THIS INFORMAL CELEBRATION WITH PLAIN WOODEN CHAIRS AND SIMPLE PLACE CARDS.

Centerpieces designed to enhance a traditional tone tend to be structured and symmetrical, featuring subdued color pairings or monochromatic schemes—not daring or bold combinations. Time-honored wedding flowers such as roses and stephanotis uphold the traditional flavor, especially when placed in classic vessels. Appropriate containers include such familiar and elegant forms as bowls, urns, and tapered vessels in gold, silver, or creamy porcelain.

If you prefer a bit more drama, you might find what you're looking for in a Victorian-style arrangement. Centerpieces in this vein evoke the romantic opulence of the nineteenth century with lavish cascades of rich burgundy, purple, and pink. Blooms are intricate and feminine—lilacs, baby's breath, and ranunculuses—and tightly packed, with an abundance of greenery spilling over stone pedestals or tumbling down golden candelabra accented with velvet ribbons. Feel free to cull from other historical eras as well, using paintings, literature, and poetry as springboards for your imagination.

RIGHT: A MOSTLY PASTEL ARRANGEMENT OF LISIANTHUS, SWEET PEAS, PEONIES, HYDRANGEAS, ROSES, AND IVY UNITES WITH STARCHED WHITE LINENS AND WHITE-PAINTED CHAIRS ON A SPACIOUS VERANDA. AS A RESULT, THE AFTERNOON RECEPTION EXUDES A FEELING OF GRACIOUS SOUTHERN STYLE AND HOSPITALITY.

OPPOSITE: TERRA-COTTA POTS FILLED WITH ROSES, PEONIES, AND LILIES INFUSE THIS TABLE WITH COUNTRY CHARM— A PERFECT LOOK FOR AN INFORMAL, OUTDOOR AFFAIR. PETALS SCATTERED ON THE TABLE AROUND THE SUN-BAKED POTS EXTEND THE DECORATIVE THEME AND ENHANCE THE CAREFREE MOOD.

If you're seeking a more casual, laid-back approach, a centerpiece with a country flair may be right up your alley. These designs—which can feature an American, French, English, or Italian slant—emphasize quaint old-fashioned charm and rustic simplicity. Best suited to informal affairs, particularly in outdoor settings, these arrangements often consist of either uncomplicated wildflowers, grasses, and herbs or unstructured tangles of blossoms, such as cabbage roses and sweet peas, that suggest the feel of an overgrown English garden. Containers that are in keeping with a country look include woven baskets, sun-baked terra-cotta pots, antique china creamers, and such farm and garden implements as seed boxes and tin buckets.

If a contemporary flair is what you're after, your centerpieces should speak of streamlined simplicity and chic minimalism. Sleek, sculpted blossoms—such as tulips, trumpet lilies, and tropical anthurium, with their distinctive waxy texture and spade shape—work best to achieve this effect; greenery might include olive branches, chosen for their scant pattern of slender green leaves. A Zenlike arrangement of carefully placed orchids and smooth stones will also bring a serene, minimalist look to your celebration.

Contemporary arrangements tend to feature one of two basic color schemes: quiet and subdued or bold and starkly contrasting. Compositions are often asymmetrical, while container shapes are highly geometric or abstract and fashioned out of anything from earthenware, stone, or wood to brushed steel or wrought iron.

OPPOSITE: AN ANTIQUE THAI
BASKET FILLED WITH PEACH
AND WHITE ROSES, PERSIM-
MONS, AND ARTICHOKES BRINGS
A TOUCH OF EXOTICISM TO
AN ALL-WHITE TABLE IN A
METROPOLITAN SETTING.
LONG, SWEEPING BRANCHES
DOTTED WITH BERRIES
EXTEND FROM THE CENTER-
PIECE LIKE OUTSTRETCHED
ARMS, ADDING AN INTRIGUING
AVANT-GARDE FLOURISH.

LEFT: A WOODEN BOX
LADEN WITH ROSES, FREESIA,
RANUNCULUSES, AND ASTILBE
IN VIVID HARVEST COLORS IS
BOTH QUAINT AND CONTEM-
PORARY—PERFECT FOR A
STYLISH AUTUMN WEDDING
IN THE COUNTRY.

RIGHT: A BLACK LACQUER TRAY HOLDS AN ABSTRACT JUNGLE CONSISTING OF POPPY PODS, MONTBRETIA, AND A SHOCKING-PINK ORCHID, ALL ENSCONCED IN A DENSE TANGLE OF WHEATGRASS AND SET AGLOW WITH VOTIVES WRAPPED IN GALAX LEAVES. ADVENTURESOME AND EVOCATIVE, A CENTERPIECE LIKE THIS MIGHT BE DESIGNED TO RECALL A FAVORITE VACATION SPOT OR TO ALLUDE TO THE HONEYMOON DESTINATION.

OPPOSITE: DAHLIAS, ORCHIDS, PRIVET BERRIES, ROSES, AND PEONIES TUMBLE OVER A TIERED PLATTER, FORMING A SORT OF DISARRAYED FLORAL PYRAMID IN THIS EXOTIC, CONTEMPORARY DESIGN. THE SOFT SPILL OF BLOOMS OFFSETS THE SHARP, ANGULAR LINES OF THE CONTAINER, WHILE GALAX-COVERED VOTIVES EXTEND THE LUSH LOOK.

RIGHT: ON THIS TASTEFUL MONOCHROMATIC TABLE, A LOOSE ARRANGEMENT OF WHITE TULIPS IN A CYLINDRICAL CRYSTAL VASE IS PLACED BETWEEN MATCHING CONTAINERS, EACH HOLDING A FLOATING CANDLE. RESTING AGAINST THE CENTERPIECE IS A CD COMPILATION OF THE BRIDE AND GROOM'S FAVORITE LOVE SONGS, GIVEN TO EACH OF THE GUESTS AS A MEMENTO. THE COVER'S SPARE DESIGN AND SANS-SERIF LETTERING BLEND HARMONIOUSLY WITH THE UNPRETENTIOUS MODERN AESTHETIC OF THE TABLE.

OPPOSITE: A GLOBE-SHAPED CRYSTAL BOWL FILLED WITH FLOATING GARDENIA BLOSSOMS AND FRINGED WITH LOOSE PETALS MAKES A CONTEMPORARY DESIGN STATEMENT IN THE MIDST OF SOFT CANDLELIGHT. ENHANCING THE FEELING OF WARMTH, A MIRRORED TRAY SET BENEATH THE BOWL REFLECTS THE MESMERIZING FLAMES. THE COLOR SCHEME OF CREAMS AND TAUPES SPEAKS OF UNDERSTATED ELEGANCE.

Centerpieces of floating blossoms and candles have also become quite popular for their ability to lend receptions a modern yet warm look. The reflection of flickering light through crystal creates an invitingly intimate yet dramatic effect.

Of course, your options are not restricted to the ones outlined here. Exotic cultures and locales, for instance, can prove to be rich sources of design motifs. There is an entire world of inspiration out there, so go with what strikes you and follow your instincts.

CHAPTER THREE

IMAGINATIVE IDEAS

PAGE 68: A LONG, RAMBLING TRAIL OF DECORATIVE SPHERES, ACCENTED WITH HURRICANE LAMPS AND SPRINKLED WITH FRAGRANT GARDENIAS, RESTS ON MOSS MATTING TO CONVEY A FEELING OF ELEGANT RUSTICITY. A DELICATE CHOCOLATE COSMOS BLOSSOM EMERGES FROM EACH NAPKIN, PROVIDING GUESTS WITH A PERSONAL WELCOME WHILE MAINTAINING THE BROWN–ON–WHITE COLOR SCHEME.

OPPOSITE: A LARGE GOLD VASE ENCRUSTED WITH A WHITE BROKEN–POTTERY MOSAIC MAKES AN EYE–CATCHING RECEPTACLE FOR AN ARRANGEMENT OF ROSES, ORCHIDS, LILIES, AND STOCK. THE VESSEL'S STRIKING MOTIF AND GENEROUS PROPOR-TIONS HELP TO BALANCE THE BOLD, NONTRADITIONAL COLOR SCHEME OF THE FLOWERS.

LEFT: AN OLD–FASHIONED HATBOX BEARING A SUMMERY DESIGN OF STRAWBERRY VINES HOLDS FRESH GARDEN ROSES AND HYDRANGEAS. ANTIQUES SHOPS AND FLEA MARKETS OFTEN PROVE TO BE TREASURE TROVES FOR COUPLES IN SEARCH OF UNUSUAL VINTAGE CONTAINERS SUCH AS THIS.

Some of the most breathtaking centerpieces result when couples let their imaginations run wild. Admittedly, it takes a certain spirit of adventure to top your reception tables with Victorian hatboxes filled to overflowing with festive blooms, birds' nests gently cradling blue candy robin's eggs, or antique cameras intermingled with framed vintage photographs. But for those willing to try some-thing new, unexpected, and perhaps even whimsical, setting off your centerpieces with out-of-the-ordinary decorative motifs can be an exciting way of providing your guests with a visual treat while expressing your personal style.

RIGHT: A HAND-SCULPTED ICE
"VESSEL" FILLED WITH ROSES
AND RASPBERRIES IS A CON-
STANTLY CHANGING WORK OF
ART THAT IS SURE TO DELIGHT
AND INTRIGUE GUESTS.

OPPOSITE: COLORFUL
GARDEN ROSES TOPPLE OVER
AN ANTIQUE SILVER TEAPOT,
CONJURING IMAGES OF
CIVILIZED AFTERNOONS IN
THE ENGLISH COUNTRYSIDE.
A NOVEL CENTERPIECE SUCH
AS THIS IS BOUND TO SPARK
CONVERSATION AMONG GUESTS.

One way of injecting your centerpieces with some originality is by being creative with the containers. Any number of unusual items can double as centerpiece
vessels, from miniature wheelbarrows and handcrafted birdhouses to extravagant ice
sculptures and gleaming silver teapots. Tree-bark bases provide a charmingly rustic
look with unusual texture, while bright blue-and-yellow majolica pitchers—particularly beautiful for outdoor receptions amid fountains and sun-drenched fruit
trees—suggest a lush Mediterranean garden.

RIGHT: THE SELECTION OF A RUSSEL WRIGHT VASE EXPRESSES AN ADMIRATION FOR MODERNIST DESIGN. IN KEEPING WITH THE PROPORTIONS AND SOOTHING SIMPLICITY OF THE VESSEL, A SMALL GROUP OF WILDFLOWERS PROVIDES A SPLASH OF COLOR WHILE MAINTAINING A SENSE OF MINIMALISM. THE CAPTIVATING CENTERPIECE JUST GOES TO SHOW THAT LESS CAN INDEED BE MORE WHEN IT COMES TO TABLE DECORATION.

OPPOSITE: WRAPPED IN PAPER HANDMADE FROM AMERICAN BARK, A LOOSE ARRANGEMENT OF APRICOT PARROT TULIPS COMMANDS ATTENTION. THE USE OF A SINGLE TYPE AND COLOR OF FLOWER LENDS A FEELING OF SOPHISTICATED ELEGANCE TO THE SETTING, AS DOES THE SINGLE SILVER CANDLESTICK PLACED ATOP EACH TABLE.

RIGHT: A TABLE SET FOR
A CHRISTMAS WEDDING
CREATES A SENSE OF MAGIC
WHEN DRAPED IN RED LINENS
AND TOPPED WITH MOUNDS OF
RED-AND-WHITE CARNATIONS.
THE FANCIFUL STRIPES OF THE
FLOWERS ARE ECHOED BY PEP-
PERMINT CANDIES SCATTERED
ACROSS THE TABLE. SHINY RED
ORNAMENTS FILL THE CENTER-
PIECE CONTAINERS AND POP UP
BETWEEN THE FLOWERS, ADDING
A LUMINOUS, REFLECTIVE
QUALITY TO THE SCENE.

OPPOSITE: CAPTURING THE
ABUNDANCE OF AN AUTUMN
HARVEST, A HOLLOWED-OUT
PUMPKIN BRIMS WITH SUN-
FLOWERS, GOLDENROD, FALL
FOLIAGE, AND OTHER COLOR-
FUL BLOOMS. THE PUMPKIN'S
TOP, TUCKED IN AMONG THE
BLOSSOMS, PROVIDES A TOUCH
OF WHIMSY, WHILE AN APPLE
GRACIOUSLY DISPLAYS THE
TABLE NUMBER.

Some couples channel their creativity into seasonal and holiday themes, which offer a wealth of opportunities for exuberant color schemes and distinctive touches. If you're planning an autumn wedding, consider hollowed-out pumpkins filled with blooms in an array of harvest colors, ranging perhaps from golden yellow to burnt orange to deep crimson. Continuing in this vein, you could accent the table with a smattering of dried autumn leaves gently sprinkled around the centerpiece or with a colorful gourd at each place setting. For a December wedding, you might turn to a festive arrangement of velvety red roses, white snowberries, holly, and deep green juniper boughs. Or you could anchor each table with a miniature topiary Christmas tree strung with twinkling white lights and placed atop cranberry red linens; to complete the effect, nestle cheerfully wrapped favors under each diminutive tree.

OPPOSITE: INSPIRED BY SCENES
ONE WOULD ENJOY DURING A
STROLL IN THE WOODS, THE
TABLE DECORATIONS AT THIS
WEDDING WERE EACH DESIGNED
WITH ONE OF THREE THEMES:
"THE FOREST FLOOR," "THE
WOODLAND STREAM," OR
"THE MEADOW." SHOWN HERE
IS "THE WOODLAND STREAM,"
CREATED WITH RIVER PEBBLES,
MOSS, MUSHROOMS, VIOLETS,
MINIATURE CATTAILS, AND
BERRIES—ALL RESTING QUIETLY
IN THE PEACEFUL SHADE OF A
DRAPING AMARANTHUS.

LEFT: "THE MEADOW" IS
TRANSPORTED TO THIS TABLE
WITH A WIDE RANGE OF
FLOWERS, HERBS, AND GRASSES,
INCLUDING OAT GRASS, CATNIP,
BASIL, LAVENDER, SEDUM,
LADY'S MANTLE, AND VIOLETS,
TO NAME A FEW. LINED WITH
WHITE CANDLES IN A VARIETY
OF SHAPES AND SIZES, THE
DISPLAY CONVEYS A SENSE
OF UNMANICURED BEAUTY
AND UNBRIDLED ROMANCE.

Valentine's Day calls for centerpieces of pink, red, and white blossoms atop bases adorned with cherubs and surrounded by chocolate kisses or conversation hearts. Another option: heart-shaped topiaries tied with pink tulle ribbon. For a wedding that falls on Halloween, consider witches' cauldrons bubbling over with blooms in orange and dusky hues (try extremely deep shades of burgundy).

Some couples weave regional themes into their centerpieces, drawing inspiration from their wedding's locale, the place they grew up, or a favorite vacation spot. A bride marrying beachside might opt for centerpieces mixing shells with flowers. Tables at an informal wedding in the American Southwest could be topped with breakaway centerpieces of painted pottery containing flowering cacti, while those in the Southeast might feature water-filled crystal bowls, each with a single perfect magnolia blossom floating inside.

RIGHT: AN ENCHANTINGLY IMAGINATIVE, NONTRADITIONAL INTERPRETATION OF THE WEDDING BANQUET INCLUDES ONE ELONGATED FLOWER-FILLED TABLE WHERE ALL GUESTS DINE TOGETHER. CHARTREUSE LINENS PROVIDE A REFRESHING BACKDROP FOR THE LONG, SWEEPING HEDGE OF BELLS OF IRELAND AND RED AND LAVENDER ROSES, WHILE A TIGHT RING OF VOTIVE CANDLES LIGHTS UP THE DISPLAY. CARRYING THROUGH THE FLORAL THEME ARE RED AND LAVENDER ROSEBUDS RESTING ON EACH GUEST'S PLATE. AT THE DOORWAY, A LEMON-LEAF GARLAND STUDDED WITH ROSES AND A PAIR OF MASSIVE URNS BRIMMING WITH BLOOMS CREATE A GRAND ENTRANCE.

OPPOSITE: TO HONOR THE GROOM'S SCOTTISH HERITAGE, WOVEN BASKETS WERE COVERED IN SCOTTISH HEATHER AND FILLED WITH CABBAGE ROSES, 'CASABLANCA' LILIES, LILACS, PINECONES, AND PEARS DECORATED WITH SILVER LEAF. A TRUE MASTERPIECE OF FLORAL DESIGN, THE CENTERPIECE IS A MARVEL TO BEHOLD.

Often, brides and grooms honor their family's heritage by including special ceremony readings, traditional dances such as the tarantella and the hora, or other old-world customs. Centerpieces, too, can offer an outlet for cultural expression. For instance, a new generation of African-American couples is reviving the custom of "jumping the broom" to symbolize crossing into a new life together; some tuck cheerfully painted miniature brooms festooned with ribbons into their centerpieces along with bows of African *kente* cloth. Similarly, some Greek-American brides sprinkle their centerpieces with sugared almonds, a traditional Greek fertility symbol that harks back to the days when marriage was expressly for the purpose of having children.

OPPOSITE: SUGARED LIMES, LEMONS, AND CANADIAN CRAB APPLES SHARE SPACE WITH YELLOW CABBAGE ROSES IN A CRYSTAL COMPOTE FOR A REFRESHING EFFECT. AT THIS ELEGANT EVENT, THE CLEVER THEME WAS CONTINUED BY SERVING CHAMPAGNE SORBET IN FROZEN GRANNY SMITH APPLES.

LEFT: A GROUPING OF VINTAGE POTTERY AND FAUX-WICKER PICNIC TINS—SET ATOP GIANT LOTUS LEAVES—BRIMS WITH RIPE PEARS, POMEGRANATES, ROSES, AND HYDRANGEAS. HEIGHTENING THE UNIQUE CHARM OF THE DISPLAY ARE AN ANTIQUE SELTZER BOTTLE IN A BRILLIANT SHADE OF TURQUOISE AND A GOLD-LEAF CAST-IRON TABLE NUMBER.

Another way to give your centerpieces a special twist is by featuring nonfloral items as the star attractions. With their gorgeous color, rich texture, and intriguing shapes, fruits and vegetables can be the sole components of an exquisite display, or they can be the primary players supported by a small cast of floral accents. A cascade of crimson pomegranates, gilded pears, and sugared grapes will create an opulent, almost regal statement to rival the most lavish of blossoms. For a summery flavor, you might fill white wicker baskets with fresh, fragrant strawberries, accented by ivy and white stephanotis blossoms—perfect for a casual garden wedding. Or stack limes and lemons in whiteware to create a dazzlingly bright, bold look against all-white tables. Since fruits and vegetables tend to cost less than flowers, they provide ample opportunity to design centerpieces that are both beautiful and affordable.

RIGHT: STANDING TALL IN THE MIDST OF A FLORAL WREATH, A SILVER-BEADED HURRICANE LAMP IS THE FOCAL POINT OF THIS TABLE. THE RING OF FLOWERS—WHICH CONSISTS OF ROSES, HYDRANGEAS, AND SWEET PEAS, AMONG OTHERS—ADDS COLOR AND TEXTURE TO THE SCENE. CELLOPHANE-WRAPPED FAVORS AND A SILVER PICTURE FRAME HOLDING THE MENU ARE THOUGHTFUL TOUCHES THAT COORDINATE WITH THE CENTERPIECE.

OPPOSITE: BERIBBONED BOXES CONTAINING GUEST FAVORS ARE DISPLAYED PROMINENTLY AROUND THE CENTERPIECE, THEREBY ENHANCING THE DEC-ORATIVE APPEAL OF THE TABLE. NOTICE HOW THE GREEN AND YELLOW SATIN BOWS PICK UP THE HUES OF THE OPULENT FLORAL WREATH SURROUNDING THE HURRICANE LAMP.

But fruits and vegetables are not the only nonfloral ingredients for eye-catching centerpieces. Look to nature's other gifts, such as seashells, pebbles, nuts, and pine-cones, for decorative help. Candles, too, offer a wealth of possibilities. While these are often used to enhance floral arrangements, they can certainly hold their own as the main feature. After all, what is more romantic than candlelight? Picture a large pillar surrounded by an ornamental wreath or a cluster of pillars in different shapes and sizes arranged in a seemingly abstract manner. A shallow, translucent bowl filled with white floating candles in the shape of snowflakes and set atop a table covered in red linens may be just the thing to give some sparkle to a winter wedding.

RIGHT: PROVIDING A STRIKING AND INEXPENSIVE ALTERNATIVE TO FLORAL ARRANGEMENTS, THE TABLE DECORATIONS AT THIS RECEPTION CONSIST OF GRANNY SMITH APPLES—SOME OF WHICH BEAR TABLE NUMBERS—AND CLUSTERS OF WHITE PILLAR CANDLES. BECAUSE THE APPLES ARE THE ONLY SPOTS OF COLOR IN THE OTHERWISE WHITE ROOM, THEY HAVE A DYNAMIC EFFECT.

OPPOSITE: BRIGHTLY COLORED GERBERA DAISIES SURROUND A LARGE GOLD MOROCCAN LANTERN THAT SITS MAJESTI-CALLY AT THE CENTER OF A SUNNY YELLOW-AND-WHITE STRIPED TABLECLOTH. EMPHASIS IS ON THE LAMP RATHER THAN THE FLOWERS, SUGGESTING THAT THE RECEPTION WILL STRETCH INTO TWILIGHT AND NIGHTFALL, WHEN THE CANDLES WILL BE LIT TO CONJURE AN ATMOSPHERE OF ROMANCE AND EXOTICISM BEFITTING THE LUSH TERRACE SETTING.

If you incorporate candles into your tabletop design, there are a few practical aspects to keep in mind. Make sure that no petals or leaves from a floral arrange-ment are at risk of falling into the flames and catching on fire. At the same time, keep votives and other candles away from the edge of the table so that guests do not knock them over by accident. If yours is an outdoor evening wedding, place candles in hurricane shades or lanterns to protect the flames from wind.

Some couples use their inventiveness to imbue their centerpieces with sym-bolism. If you're seeking to give your table decorations special meaning, design them to reflect your interests or something that is important to you. Perhaps you and your spouse-to-be fell in love as university students and still spend Saturday afternoons rooting for your alma mater in every sport; if this is the case, why not create arrangements that proudly display your college colors? If baking is your

passion and you dream of opening a restaurant, cluster beautiful loaves of bread amid decorative bottles of olive oil as a centerpiece. Couples who love antiques often comb flea markets for vintage silver picture frames, candlesticks, and other treasures, then create centerpieces from their personal collection. (If you plan to do this, be sure your florist attaches a note to the bottom of each centerpiece informing guests that the containers are not to be taken home with them when they leave.)

Finding the right centerpiece design is much like finding the perfect gown or the ideal setting for your wedding. You most likely want it to reflect your taste, personality, and sense of style. Whether you find your inspiration in this book, at a festive event, or in some aspect of your life, the most important guideline to follow is whether or not the arrangements feel right to you. So go with your instincts, and take the opportunity to have some fun.

RIGHT: SYMBOLIZING PROS-
PERITY AND ABUNDANCE, A
LIVE GOLDFISH IS THE MAIN
ATTRACTION OF THIS CENTER-
PIECE. AT THE END OF THE
EVENING, ONE LUCKY GUEST
FROM EACH TABLE TAKES
HOME A NEW PET.

OPPOSITE: DECORATIVE
MONARCH BUTTERFLIES
HOVER OVER AN ARRANGE-
MENT OF ROSES IN PALE
SUNSET COLORS, PLUMP
BERRIES, AND MEANDERING
TRAILS OF GREENERY. FAVORS
WRAPPED IN SHEET MUSIC ADD
A PERSONAL TOUCH, REFLECT-
ING A PASSION FOR THE ARTS.

RIGHT AND OPPOSITE:
PROVIDING A MOUTH-
WATERING ALTERNATIVE
TO FLORAL CENTERPIECES,
A COUPLE HAS DECKED EVERY
TABLE WITH A SMALL CAKE
POISED ON A BED OF FLOWERS.
EACH DESSERT BEARS A SPECIAL
MESSAGE, SUCH AS "LAUGHTER"
OR "JOY." FOR A PLAYFULLY
ROMANTIC TOUCH, CANDY
HEARTS ARE SCATTERED
ACROSS THE TABLES.

Avi Adler
87 Luquer Street
Brooklyn, NY 11231
tel: 718-243-0804
www.aviadler.com

Castle & Pierpont
401 East 76th Street
New York, NY 10021
tel: 212-570-1284
www.castleandpierpont.com

Floramor Studios
569 Seventh Street
San Francisco, CA 94103
tel: 415-864-0145
www.floramor.com

Susan Holland
142 Fifth Avenue, 4th floor
New York, NY 10011
tel: 212-807-8892
www.susanholland.com

J. Gordon Designs
146 West 29th Street, 6E
New York, NY 10001
tel: 212-563-1138

Leslie Palme Event Design
24 Fiske Place, #3
Brooklyn, NY 11215
tel: 718-622-6995

Magnolia
Jennifer Pfeiffer
New York, NY
tel: 212-243-7302
by appointment only

Bette Matthews
Brooklyn, NY
tel: 718-857-4699
bettematthews@aol.com
by appointment only

Renny Designs for Entertaining
505 Park Avenue
New York, NY 10022
tel: 212-288-7000

Elizabeth Ryan
411 East 9th Street
New York, NY 10009
tel: 212-995-1111

SBK Associates, Floral Decorators
3 East 63rd Street, Suite #1C
New York, NY 10021
tel: 212-813-0251

Stanlee R. Gatti Designs
1208 Howard Street
San Francisco, CA 94103
tel: 415-558-8884
www.stanleegatti.com

Tapestry, Bridal & Special Event Flowers
842 Rhode Island Street
San Francisco, CA 94107
tel: 415-550-1015
www.tapestryflowers.com

Two Design Group
1937 Irving Blvd., Suite A
Dallas, TX 75207
tel: 214-741-3145

Verdure
3014 Benvenue Avenue
Berkeley, CA 94705
tel: 510-548-7764

Avi Adler: p. 76 (photo ©Susie Montagna)

©Paul Barnett: pp. 43, 59, 87

©Pat Bluestein: p. 90 (arrangement by Barbara Shack)

Castle & Pierpont Event Design: pp. 28 (photo ©Harold Hechler Associates), 51, 58, 64 (photo ©Harold Hechler Associates), 65 (photo ©Harold Hechler Associates), 57

©Joshua Ets-Hokin: p. 49 (flowers by Verdure)

Susan Holland: pp. 2, 37, 42 (photo ©Andrea Sperling), 62, 71 (photo ©Andrea Sperling), 72, 73, 74, 75, 83

©Karen Hill: pp. 23, 53

©Eliot Hotlzman: pp. 25 (flowers by Stanlee Gatti), 38 (flowers by Stanlee Gatti), 40 (flowers by Stanlee Gatti), 44 (flowers by Stanlee Gatti), 45 (flowers by Stanlee Gatti), 47 (flowers by Gretchen Lawton), 52 (flowers by Stanlee Gatti), 78 (flowers by Floramor), 79 (flowers by Floramor), 80 (flowers by Stanlee Gatti)

©Roy Llera: pp. 26, 66, 85, 92, 93

©Lyn Hughes: pp. 8 (flowers by Belle Fleur), 20, 21, 86

©Harold Hechler Associates: pp. 15 (flowers by J. Gordon Designs), 67

J. Gordon Designs: pp. 22, 60, 61

©Sarah Merians: p. 18

©Antonio Rosario: pp. 1 (flowers by Magnolia), 11 (flowers by Bette Matthews), 30 (flowers by Magnolia)

Elizabeth Ryan: pp. 32, 63

Renny Designs for Entertaining: pp. 34, 35 top, 35 bottom

SBK Associates, Floral Decorators: pp. 27 (photo ©Fred Marcus), 48 (photo ©Fred Marcus)

©Andrea Sperling: pp. 16, 41

Tapestry, Bridal & Special Event Flowers: pp. 19 (photo ©Peter Diggs), 24 (photo ©Martina Konietzny), 31, 33, 36, 50, 54, 55 (photo ©Martina Konietzny), 56 (photo ©Jan Lundburg), 68 (photo ©Juliet Varnedoe), 70, 84 (photo ©Michelle Walker)

Two Design Group: pp. 3, 12, 81, 82

Verdure: pp. 46 (photo ©Suzanne Parker), 88, 91

©Therese Marie Wagner: pp. 6 (flowers by DeJuan Stroud), 29 (flowers by Leslie Palme Event Design), 77, 89